# Solstice

Christopher J. Arthur

Leaf by Leaf is an imprint of Cinnamon Press.
www.cinnamonpress.com

 ISBN 978-1-78864-938-4

British Library Cataloguing in Publication Data. A CIP record for this book can be obtained from the British Library.



Designed and typeset in Bodoni by Cinnamon Press. Cover design by Adam Craig.

Cinnamon Press is represented by Inpress Ltd.

# Author Biography

Born in 1940, Christopher J. Arthur studied at the Universities of Nottingham (1959-63) and Oxford (1963-65). He then gained a post at the newly-formed University of Sussex, teaching philosophy in the School of Social Sciences for many years. He took up poetry only after his retirement from teaching. He continues to live in Brighton with his partner, Morag.

In his student days Chris Arthur was active in the Campaign for Nuclear Disarmament. Later he  was a founding member of the Radical Philosophy Group, and he served as an editor of its journal *Radical Philosophy*. Also, for some time he was on the jury awarding the Deutscher Memorial Prize annually, for books in or about the Marxist tradition.

He has published many scholarly papers, and he authored three books: *Dialectics of Labour* (Basil Blackwell 1986), *The New Dialectic and Marx's 'Capital'* (Brill 2002), and *The Spectre of Capital* (Brill 2022).

# Contents

# Preface

Poetry occupies a space between prose and music. Like prose it has cognitive content; and it may present ideas and experiences in fresh and striking imagery. Like music it has a soundscape; it features rhythm and harmony.

In building a soundscape the poet has an extensive toolbox to hand. There is metre, rhyme, consonance, assonance, onomatopoeia, and much more. To register these effects poetry must be read aloud.

It is often remarked that the stresses in natural English give rise to iambic words and phrases. Hence the prevalence (in the past at least) of such metrical schemes as iambic pentameter. The pentameter line is long enough to contain a complex idea, but short enough to deliver in a breath. Not only may a line be metrically sound, but an entire poem may itself have a formal shape, as with the sonnet. The first poem below is a text-book Shakespearean sonnet (with metatextuality thrown in as a bonus); but there is no necessity to stick to such formal structure; thereafter even poems that look like sonnets at first glance turn out to be irregular.

Today poetry may be obtained etherially; but I belong to the generation that values still the solidity of an artefact, to wit a book. So I present this chapbook for perusal.

I thank for their encouragement and advice, at various times, Morag McCall-Smith, Naomi Foyle, Colin Davies, Alexander McCall Smith, Tim Devlin, and Claire Crowther.

I also thank Jan Fortune of Leaf by Leaf for her prompt attention to my manuscript.

for Morag

# Solstice

## On Being Set A Sonnet

Now prides the Autumn on her days, I turn
to pen her fire, in hope I have the skill
to make these days of Autumn blaze and burn
in written form — but find my hand is still.
How *shall* a sonnet seed itself, and swell
to ripened form, when there is little chance
of finding words that work, that serve to spell
my meanings out in lines that, partnered, dance?
Before the season's passed, I scratch some tries
at shapely lyric verse, which scans and rhymes,
which holds the present fast before it dies,
obedient to Nature's turning times.
Though still my hand's uncertain, all the same
a poem buds, and blooms! — now Pride's aflame.

## On the Night Side of the World

Midnight; the watchful moon's now gone to ground;
I lie alone; time's turning wheel is still.
They say: we all sleep under the same sky.
But is it really true? For — I and you —
we're so far apart, that you're loud with light,
and I am fretful, in the frowning dark.

(*apologies to Sappho*)

## Sappho's Reproof

You loved not poetry; you never sought
for the sacred spring below Olympus,
to lie beside the roses gathered there;
you ever shall go unremembered then,
and flit among a host of Shades unsung.

(*after Sappho*)

## Solstice

Remember Sherbrook, pure and cold,
and a shallow sun, grown old?
Besieged by frozen furze, and wearied by the wind,
we halted, and sealed … ourselves … in a kiss.

Cold clings to my kitchen;
but the scarlet amaryllis on the sill's
blooming obscenely;
a robin fights his double in the glass.
Your verse about a blackbird hops into my head,
and one about a fallen goat, forever dead;
the 'x's on your mails … as fresh as grass.

A crisp attack of cramp in the night-time
… passes. — And where are you?
Are you warm, I wonder, where you are?

## The Lost Village

Deep in the Downs no sign is seen
of hidden homes in fields folded;
no infant sprawls upon the sward;
no tolling bell tells of the dead,
for even death itself is fled
now ev'ry soul's departed. Yet,
if nothing of a nave remains,
where once a people knelt and prayed,
still their stories trouble the brooding earth,
beneath these sky-borne larks, rejoicing.

## Is this the path?

There was a man who sought to find himself,
and roamed through many lands where he might be,
till he caught a face mirrored in a pool;
but who is he, he asked himself, who seeks?
He then looked back at his meand'ring path,
the trace his tread made on the way ahead,
and, laughing, strode off down the road once more:
himself, just as he always was before.

## On Hopper's *Sun in an empty room*

A wash of sunlight floods an empty room;
it enters through a window to the right,
and stamps a glowing oblong on the floor,
unoccupied for now, but once
a thinnish woman, posing there,
took off her orange dress and stood up bare.
   Yet nothing is spoken; all is implied.

Once you were happy. (When he kissed you.)
Now, you advertise yourself,
and sit at a bar by a stranger's side.
But know this: it matters not who you are,
nor what particular hurt you carry,
what the tiring office stair you tread, the
droning laundromat wherein you tarry;
for you can always open wide
your window to the sun, and let
its universal benediction claim you,
let it find this empty heart you hide;
unclothed you'll stand, as if made new,
of every shadow shorn, and full
   of light!

## New Year Eve

Close-handed through the dark, my love and I
follow our friends along a puddled road,
heading, over unseen rushing burns, for
a festive light at Morven Hall, and wine.

## Tobermory

The mountains were cradling a winter sun,
the day we went to Tobermory.
Our boat biffed the swell of the sea,
and we sailed up a paint-boxed street,
when we went to Tobermory.
With stores piled high,
and racing a darkening sky,
back we came — from Tobermory.

## Bladderwrack

Slowly, along the loch, the creeping sea
swallows a rocky shore,
then just as slowly gives it back,
adorned with all the wrack and bladder of
its secret peristaltic life.

# A Later Look at London

Night folds her faded wings, and falls away;
the first few birds are stirring on the Heath.
A sudden dawning reds the rim of day,
and stains the city skyline's broken teeth.
The trains return to life, and thread their way
through silver veins that worm the earth beneath.
A morning chorus — shrilled alarms from clocks —
calls to their ordained treadmills Moloch's priests;
penned in their stations row on row like beasts,
they cycle, and recycle, bonds and stocks.
The river rides the tides that never sleep;
embanked on ev'ry side against his will,
a looped intestine swerves his waters' sweep.
S'int Paul's great skull sits proud upon its hill,
above the stream advancing on the Deep;
and all 'that mighty heart' is beating; still.

(*apologies to William Wordsworth*)

## Perhaps

He'd met her by chance, at his bickering flat;
— a party for refugees, from Chile perhaps,
supported by the Unions, and the University,
a mixed crowd, some students, some not.
And there she was. (Talking too loud.)
Removed from the hubbub he watched her intently.
He liked her, her loudness, her lightness, her laugh.
Would she smile, and say *Do I know you?* Would she stay?
Was this his long-awaited love, perhaps?
She had seen him, standing there, seeing her;
and they talk through the night, in his flickering flat.
Is it love? Almost. Perhaps. We shall see,
in the next instalment of the story,
playing itself out — to end, perhaps, in glory?

## On First Looking into Hegel's 'Logic'

— Not for Hegel vague effusions of the Heart!
Spirit, purged of Sense, takes Logic for its part.
'Being', 'Nothing', and 'Becoming', enter thought
on a count of three; for Being—So is but
coming so to be from what it sets at naught.
All such Notions co-defined, their circle's shut.
Like a frieze of figures on a Grecian urn
forever caught in clay, serenely posed are they.
But see! They lift their skirts, they twist and turn,
they're dancing — dancing! Swirling to the sway
of Spirit's 'trancing beat, they weave the world.
I, too, entranced. — As moved, by this philosophy,
in which the Universal Mind is made to speak,
as old Balboa, 'top a continental peak,
when he — soul soaring — spied a boundless sea.

(*apologies to John Keats*)

## Tracey's Bed

Her unmade bed
sprawled shameless to the sight;
her stocking torn, her coffee spilt,
her sheet no longer white.
*She made her mark, that one,*
remarked the maid who set it right,
shook her out, swept her up,
and tucked her corners tight.
But to the unmaking of many beds
there came no end, until the night
when her unmaking went itself unmade;
of her, day brought no trace to light.

## Love's friend

Poetry is ever Love's friend,
a poem for the start of it,
another for the end.

## The Return

The turning world takes her,
in turn returns her. Oh! the kisses!

# Caged

The soul is a seabird,
cribbed in a cage, wings
beating — beating.
The breast at its last breathing
ghosts the brush of something leaving
— leaving.
A broken cage lies
shattered on the shore
whilst on his bride the sea
there rides a great white bird,
preening.
So shall we be
but a bird-beat caged, wings
weeping — (weeping).

## A Cloak of Stars

The night wears a cloak of stars.
Venús, Jupiter, and Mars,
a host! — sewn on velvet dark —
unfold, spark by glowing spark.

## The Fallen

Rank on rank the trees bend to the wind like reeds;
gales unhorse the chestnuts from their flailing steeds;
bursting shells, across a conquered field,
gape their wounded flesh, and beauty yield.

## Buckstones

bright water jumps
through cleftèd stone
steeps deep and cold
bare bathers bold

## Why do we come to these graves?

*(for Joe)*

Why come we to these graves? Why linger?
— when the hollow at the heart remains,
— when spelling out his name
won't bring him back again,
and stay these sighs.

There are no resurrections to be drawn
from all this squared-off grass.
These stones will never morph
to living flesh, and laugh
at our surprise.

Who are all these flowers for, exactly?
(They're left beside a house where he's not home.)
But, still, I'm pleased to see
how graceful is the stone
that lids his eyes.

Its face relays a line of Yeats'
chosen by his widow; but not the line
he chose himself one time,
which she forgot, thinking it not
... important ... yet.

So, we come, with or without our flowers,
here, to these graves, rememb'ring those we loved,
and the hours, too few, they had with us.

## The ‘Tank Man’ of Tiananmen Square

— Clean underwear.
His mother always mentioned that.
*And what if you were knocked down in the road?*
 she’d ask.
— But not his best blue trousers;
 they might be needed, later.
(*They are coming. They are coming.*)
— And, most important, a fresh white shirt;
 so like a bride.
(*They shall not pass.*)
— No coat. No cap.
A tank comes growling up the street.
Step out; stand straight;
meet the faceless, face to fate:
 *Here … I … stay!*

# Autumn

Flurries of sudden rain
stipple the gutter pool,
clouding an imaged sky
held in the water's eye.

A gusty breeze makes tattered birds
of 'papers piled in passageways,
whirls them wildly along the High,
and cedes them, lying, cast away,
undone in dying disarray.

Above the fields, a feathered arrowhead
is flying, aimed at bowers overseas;
their blood run back to earth, the failing leaves
disrobe again a stand of silent trees;
the stations of the sun are shrinking fast,
these last days of the season filing past.

The year has changed her weight toward the other pole.
Summer's stride now spent, Winter's takes the leading role.

## What Will You Remember?

*What will you remember,*
when nothing's turned out as you planned?
— the curve of a woman under your hand;
the overwhelming scent of jasmine in the night;
and swimming to the moon along a trail of light.

*What will you remember?*
— a great cathedral's walls resound
to Mozart's Requiem, in which you drowned.

*What will you remember?*
— the love you sought, so nearly found,
your still-born kisses scattered on the ground.

*What will you remember,*
now you have lost your promised land?
— a shout … a fall … a marching band,
a bank of lilies gathered round
an altar with your desolation crowned.

## Haiku

early plum blossom
decks bare branches — clings on
though the wind turns north

## taking time

wound-up by the springs of youth
wound-down by the time we spend
the heart beating time is beaten by time
        in the end

## Anon. ’e must be …

Anon. ’as written such a lot.
But not, alas, late—ly.
Alack! ’e must lie in ’is plot.
I’ll not miss ’im great—ly.

## Written in the Stars

Is God the mothership of all the stars,
strange missionaries sent into the dark
to code a testament in punctured night,
for all to see? But since we lack the key
what zodiac can cast its signs aright,
what prism re-refract this splintered light?
The stars are spread across the universe,
reconstellated as each point of view
defines their varied lexicon anew.
How could the Wise Men know that sudden spark
might also mark the birth of she who came —
far off in Space — to save an alien race.
But nothing may be read from heaven's face;
in truth, this screen of stars does not compute;
it is no window sharing files that show
their future to the fated here below.

## Beach

Imagine — all the dead souls on the beach —
they think they live because they move
— the stones — these ever-moving stones
moved by the surging sea.
If some are thrown up higher than the rest
what then?
As the waters move with the moon
they are but drowned again — the stones —
under the swelling sea.
But still they rise anew — the dead —
to lifeless life once more;
these ever-stirring stones — they shape —
this ever-shifting shore
— these stones —
these sursurrating stones.
At ev'ry flowing tide — the stones —
this shingle wall restore
as wave on wave they join
the souls that rose before
— the stones — these ever-moving stones.

## The Stones

We stood against the Western wind, untamed,
at our accustomed places, lapped the dew,
saw passing dragons hide behind the clouds.
Men came; intent, implacable, inflamed,
they tore us roughly from our native ground.

— Borne over water first, I think, and then
pulled over land, until we settled here,
met with our neighbour (we were kin of course),
shoulder to shoulder held a third aloft,
and kept our stations on this templed plot.

Abandoned, we yet endured, still survived,
though when the earth was shaken many fell,
and centuries left scars across our sides.
Form decayed and meaning bled, we waited,
till men came to rue what time has fated.

In orbit round us, daily they parade,
some with shouts and laughter, but some in sil-
ent contemplation, in their courses stayed;
here's one that rests, and dreams with us the while.

## The Plague Year

By the rules of separation,
at my sea-skirted home,
the voices of my friends
now absented, I can but wait,
wait for this empty year to end,
should it … end.

While people fall, like the leaves fall
that mar the paving stones,
they quarrel at the court.
One saw fit to make a journey
when no journey was to be made;
and as he quit the palace gate,
behind him, falling leaves
littered a granite courtyard's floor.
Now he himself has fallen, and he rides
past all the ruined castles of the North
unto his place of exile by the Wall.

And still I wait, wait for it all to pass;
should it ever
… pass.

*(Apologies to Alexander McCall Smith,*
*who put Dom Cummings in a pastiche Tang poem)*

# Clap for Carers

In that unwonted time of separation,
suspended in our bubble, we floated,
staged a simulacrum of life on screens,
though vile deaths yet flickered there, vicariously.

At dusk,
a trumpet sounded when the Clap began.
Along the shuttered street, amazingly,
the doors gave birth to people, scores of them,
and all applauding where they stand.
We waved to neighbours whom we hardly knew,
felt good about ourselves,
for giving thanks when thanks were due.

So did you clap; or did your saucepan sing;
what contribution to the clamour did you bring?

# When (Song)

We shall have torn the forest from the flowers,
when only paper roses bloom for us.
We shall have seen the swallows year on year depleted,
when in time the last one falls by us.

We shall have heard the wind shriek through the towers,
when, long before, they still stood over us.
We shall have drained the boiling seas of all their fishes,
when they take our ground from under us.

We shall have found the soil-rows lose their powers,
when nothing grows so greenly tall to us.
We shall have met the lurid spaceman at his landing,
when we see him then recoil from us.

We shall have scorched our skins with acid showers,
when all our burning eyes stare back at us.
We shall have eaten all the Earth, and all that's on it,
when we eat Ourselves (what's left of us).

## Time ... and Time Again

I

Before the world awoke to Time
nothing was set, determined, fixed,
'so', and not 'so'.
But then — bang — all became just as it is,
and not some other thing altogether
— which might have been as good,
or, maybe, not,
different anyhow,
with only one sun in the sky.

II

Do not say: Time has cast the past away.
My past is still with me,
though not with all my other futures bright
that never came to be.
Those were the times Time cast aside;
the unlived lives it sacrificed for mine.

## Notes on the Poems

Sappho's Reproof:
The Pierian spring sacred to the Muses, crowned with its roses, is at the base of Mount Olympus

Solstice:
Sherbrook is a brook on Cannock Chase.

The Lost Village:
Balsdean was inhabited until the Second World War, when the population was evacuated and the buildings were used for artillery practice. These were never rebuilt, and the people never returned. A slate marks the site of the vanished chapel.

On Hopper's *Sun in an Empty Room*:
This poem refers to several of Edward Hopper's pictures. In *Sun in an Empty Room* (1963), one of his last paintings, his fundamental subject finally comes into sole focus; not a figure bathed in light but the light itself. The 'oblong', however, is in another late picture, *A Woman in the Sun* (1960); a naked woman (his wife) is standing in it. No 'orange dress' is visible, but we know from other pictures it was a favourite of hers: see for example *Morning Sun* (1952). The 'bar' is in *Nighthawks* (1942) of course. The 'laudromat' is, in fact, *Automat* (1927). For an 'office' see *Office at Night* (1942). This transcendental role of light is light not absorbed in itself but ready to receive us into its embrace.

Beach:
'sursurrating' is a deliberate adaptation of susurrating.

www.ingramcontent.com/pod-product-compliance
Ingram Content Group UK Ltd.
Pitfield, Milton Keynes, MK11 3LW, UK
UKHW042009190726
13854UKWH00005B/2229

9 781788 649636